String Time Jogg

14 pieces for flexible ensemble

Kathy and David Blackwell

MUSIC DEPARTMENT

OXFORD
UNIVERSITY PRESS

OXFORD
UNIVERSITY PRESS

Great Clarendon Street, Oxford OX2 6DP, England
198 Madison Avenue, New York, NY 10016, USA

Oxford University Press is a department of the University of Oxford.
It furthers the University's aim of excellence in research, scholarship,
and education by publishing worldwide

Oxford is a registered trade mark of Oxford University Press
in the UK and in certain other countries

9 10

ISBN 978-0-19-335916-1

Music and text origination by
Barnes Music Engraving Ltd., East Sussex
Printed in Great Britain on acid-free paper by
Halstan & Co. Ltd., Amersham, Bucks.

All pieces are original compositions by the authors unless stated otherwise.

Contents

Introduction

String Time Joggers is a collection of flexible ensemble pieces for young string players at the level of the *Joggers* books for violin, viola, and cello. This pack contains the score, a separate piano part, and a CD. There are separate books with parts for violin, viola, cello, and double bass.

Parts

Each piece has music for Parts 1 and 2—both of which can be played by violin, viola, and cello—a double bass part, and a piano part. In some pieces there are optional extra parts (see below).

Part 1 is for pupils around the end of *Joggers* and uses all fingers in the pattern 0–1–2–34 for violin and viola and 0–1–34 for cello.

Part 2 is for pupils at the start of *Joggers* and uses open strings and first fingers only.

In some pieces there are slight differences in these parts so that the violin can use the E string and the viola and cello the C string. These are all shown in the score with separate stems or different staves.

Optional **extra parts** are given for the three pieces of the Jamaican Suite: a harmony part for the outer pieces and a descant for the middle piece. These all require all fingers to be used in the same pattern as Part 1.

An optional **double bass part** is provided for each piece. This is largely an independent bass line, though elements of Parts 1 and 2 are used. Each part uses the finger pattern 0–1–4, with the exception of 'Kingston Calypso' and 'Cowboy song' which also use second finger. We are grateful to Tom Morter for his help with writing the double bass parts.

Finally, a **piano part** is provided. Either this or the backing track on the CD is required for each piece.

The **score** shows all the different parts for each piece, but to keep the music uncluttered and clear, Parts 1 and 2 are usually shown at violin and viola pitch and in the treble clef; it is understood that these parts are doubled an octave lower by cellos.

Scoring options

The pieces can be played in all kinds of ways to suit the group available, from duets in any combination to large ensembles. With the exception of 'Broadway or bust', the pieces can also be played as solos with piano accompaniment. The double bass part can be omitted, as can Part 2 if necessary (with the exception of 'Broadway or bust'). Different instruments could be allotted to the different parts or, for a richer effect, parts could be split between all the instruments. The optional extra parts in the Jamaican Suite provide further possibilities for larger or more confident groups.

CD

The CD contains a performance and backing track for each piece. The performances illustrate the range of performance options available. Extra percussion or a drumkit is added to some of the backing tracks. We are grateful to the following musicians for playing on the CD: Olivier Bonnici, Jane Griffiths, Barney Morse-Brown, Colin Fletcher, and Tom Hooper.

 This symbol indicates the CD track numbers for each piece. The top number indicates the complete performance, and the bottom number the accompaniment alone. A tuning note (A) is located on track 29.

Teacher's Notes

The following pages contain short notes on each piece, with ideas for warm-up activities, things to listen out for, performance ideas, and suggestions for extending the material in different ways. These are intended as starting-points, and can be used at will and developed to suit the group. Taking a rhythm or some technical point from the pieces being learnt and incorporating it into a simple warm-up activity is an effective way of learning and makes good use of often limited rehearsal time.

Suites and Extras

The pieces are arranged in four suites of three pieces each, to provide an instant concert programme, but choose and play the pieces in any combination. There are also two 'extra' pieces, providing simple material suitable for warm ups or workshops or encores. Many of the pieces were written for the junior string players of Kidlington Area Music School, Oxfordshire, and we hope will be enjoyed by all young string groups.

Teacher's Notes

Sea Suite

Shark attack!

Warm up 1: Work on dynamics to create a real feeling of excitement. Play the rhythm of bars 6–9 on an open string and encourage a build in dynamics from p to f. Say 'shark bite' on the accented notes to help get the character of the piece.

Warm up 2: Try the same thing for bars 18–21, this time with a diminuendo and no accents.

Listen out 1: In Part 1 encourage a good tunnel shaped left hand, with 3rd finger (4th for cellos) held down through bars 6/7, 10/11, etc.

Listen out 2: Make sure the rhythm of the final bar is quavers!

Performing: The notes in Part 2 bars 4–5 can be played double stopped or *divisi*.

Ideas: Improvise an atmospheric introduction with some snap pizzicato on open Gs or Ds over a tremolo G on the piano.

Barrier Reef

Warm up 1: With the backing track alone, do some pizzicato strumming on open strings, encouraging large free movements in the right hand. The pizzicato should be gentle, slow, and over the fingerboard, with the upper strings' right hand drawing a circle in the rests. Cellists could think about drawing a rugby ball shape in the air as they strum with their thumb diagonally from G to A strings. The aim is to sound 'watery' like bubbles in a snorkel! Alternatively, the upper strings could try strumming with their left hand; place the left hand in middle position and let the left arm move freely from the shoulder.

Warm up 2: Practise switching from pizz. to arco (Part 2). Younger players may prefer to put the bow down for the pizzicato section and pick it up again for the arco section at letter [A]. It is worth practising this, giving time to reform a good bow hold.

Listen out: Encourage quiet and gentle playing making sure that it doesn't get too loud.

Performing: The final harmonic in Part 1 could be optional—play a stopped D instead. Add a rain stick for some atmospheric sound effects; alternatively, players could imitate the gentle sound of the sea lapping on the shore with a quiet 'shhhh!' through the introduction and the two bars rest before letter [B].

Ideas: Choose the backing track alone and improvise on the G pentatonic scale starting on D (D E G A B). Two-bar phrases can be invented by teacher or pupil to be copied back or answered.

Cap'n Jack's Hornpipe

Warm up 1: Play the rhythm of bar 7 on each note of the D scale.

Warm up 2: Teach everyone how to count multi-rests.

Listen out: Make sure bars 30–1 in Part 1 are 'tidy'; the note before letter [B] needs to be short.

Performing: A full string ensemble could contrast *tutti* and *solo* sections by choosing soloists or a small group for bars 23–38. If your group can manage it, aim for a fast tempo with a strong feel of two in a bar. Add some pirate props and costumes for an end of term performance.

Ideas: Listen to some recordings of music inspired by the sea or water. Improvise a sound effects piece about a calm or a stormy sea. Explore harmonics, *tremolo* bowings, dynamics, *col legno*, pizz., etc.

Jazz Suite

Simple syncopation

Warm up 1: To help Part 1 with the syncopation, clap the rhythm of bar 3 using these words, 'let's play this jazzy tune'.

Warm up 2: In the same way, practise the rhythm of Part 2 at letter **A** with the words 'let's play it now!'

Listen out 1: Make sure that the crotchets in Part 2 aren't held on through the rests.

Listen out 2: Bars 13 and 17 of the violin Part 1 may need some extra practice.

Performing: Part 1 splits in bars 11–18, with an E string part for the violins and a separate part for the violas and cellos.

Ideas: Add some percussion to *lift* the performance. In the first and last sections try finger clicks or a triangle on beats two and four; at letter **A** try playing the rhythm of Part 2 on tambourine.

Feelin' blue

Warm up: Make everyone aware of bow direction and practise re-taking the bow on some open string notes; encourage a free circular movement of the right hand.

Listen out: Check that everyone understands *divisi*.

Performing: If Part 2 in the opening section is played in unison, choose the lower notes. If playing in parts with a full string ensemble, split Part 2 between violins and violas on the upper notes and cellos on the lower notes; it then works best if Part 1 is played by the upper strings. Point out that the tune is in Part 2 at letter **A**. Add a pause on the final chord. If players can manage the switch, the double bass could play pizzicato at letter **A**, returning to arco on the D.S.

Ideas: Invent some lyrics to fit the rhythm. Part 1 could start with 'Tell me are you feelin' blue?' (bars 3–4), with Part 2 answering 'Yes I'm feelin' blue.' Letter **A** could be 'I hate homework', etc.

Broadway or bust

Warm up 1: Teach the first section by rote in a call and response style, playing four notes at a time. Split the players into two groups and play as written.

Warm up 2: Practise the final tremolo note, encouraging a relaxed bow hold.

Listen out: Encourage a good pizzicato sound at letter **B** with plucking over the fingerboard. Either right or left hand could be used for the pizzicato; upper strings can use 4th finger (left hand in middle position) and the cellos could alternate their 3rd and 4th fingers, alternating one bar of each.

Performing: This has to be played in two parts. In a full string ensemble the best result will be achieved with all the upper strings playing Part 1 and the lower strings on Part 2. Make sure the quavers are swung in the piano part. Structurally, the piece is a 12-bar blues, with 4 choruses following a short piano introduction. You could mark this structure with different scorings for the different choruses.

Ideas: In the outer sections add some finger clicks or percussion on beats two and four. At a concert invite the audience to join in and do this—this might take some rehearsal!

Jamaican Suite

Tinga Layo

Warm up 1: Play the rhythm of bar 5 on each note of the D scale using these words, 'have a banana'.

Warm up 2: Split your players into two groups and play a scale of D as a round, like this:

Listen out: Check that the two successive up bows in bars 20 and 24 are observed.

Performing: The harmony part is optional. If performing with a full string ensemble divide the upper strings on Part 1 and the harmony line while all the lower strings play Part 2. The piano accompaniment could be optional.

Ideas: Try adding some percussion. A tambourine playing the rhythm of bar 5 would add some colour.

Jamaican lullaby

Warm up 1: Play the rhythm of bar 5 on each note of the scale of D using the word 'Rastafarian'.

Warm up 2: Play a scale of D slurring two notes to a bow.

Listen out 1: Check that the rhythm of bar 17 is correct—it's the one bar with a different syncopated pattern.

Listen out 2: Encourage a 'singing' tone in the descant line; make everyone aware of bow division and speed.

Performing: The descant part is optional. If it is used, omit the first time and add the second time through. The repeat of the introduction will give players time to 'gather' and switch to the descant line.

Ideas: Split Part 1 into two groups and play the tune through in two-bar sections, the first group playing the first two bars, then handing over to the second group for the next two bars (and so on). Can players join the tune together smoothly? Split Part 2 into two and try the same thing with both parts.

Kingston Calypso

Warm up 1: Teach the rhythm of bars 5–6 with the words 'If you want to play a nice calypso'; clap it and play it on an open string or to a scale of G.

Warm up 2: In the same way, teach the rhythm at letter C with these words 'mangoes and coconuts'.

Listen out: Make sure that the crotchets in bars 14–16 and 18–20 are short and not held on through the rests. Quietly saying 'shh, shh' in the rests can be helpful.

Performing: The optional harmony part is for upper strings only. The viola and cello Part 2 is different from the violin Part 2 and uses the C string (the viola part of course sounds an octave higher than as notated in the score). If performing with a full string ensemble, try varying the orchestration at letter C; for example, bars 29–36 could be upper strings only with everyone joining in at D.

Ideas: Add some claves or other dry percussion playing this 3+3+2 rhythm:

Hollywood Suite

Spy movie 2

Warm up 1: Play the rhythm of bar 13 on a scale or on open strings.

Warm up 2: Play the rhythm at letter [B] on an open D making sure the final quaver is not held on through the rests and has an accent.

Listen out 1: Make sure everyone understands multi-rests.

Listen out 2: Work on a tidy ending. Encourage everyone to count the rests and watch for the final pizzicato note.

Performing: Younger players may prefer to play the opening pizzicato without their bow in hand—there is time in the multi-rest before letter [A] to pick it up and re-shape a good bow hold.

Ideas: Listen to some recordings of film music. Create some music for a scary film—a haunted house or a space adventure might provide inspiration.

Sad movie

Warm up 1: Practise the slurs by playing a scale of D, slurring two notes to a bow.

Warm up 2: To help Part 1 with bow division, repeat bars 5–6 a few times encouraging whole bows every two beats.

Listen out 1: Make sure there is a neat re-take of the bow at letter [B].

Listen out 2: Encourage good tone quality on the semibreves with the use of whole bows and awareness of bow speed.

Performing: The slurs in Part 2 could be optional.

Ideas: Add some gentle percussion, such as Indian bells.

Action movie

Warm up 1: Play the rhythm of bar 5 on each note of the D arpeggio.

Warm up 2: Play the triplet rhythm of Part 2, bar 14 on an open D string using these words 'knock at the door'.

Warm up 3: Practise playing crotchet open Ds pizzicato with the bow held in the hand.

Listen out: Check that the up bows at the beginning of phrases always start in the middle of the bow and not at the tip.

Performing: The pizzicato at letter [C] could be optional.

Ideas: Include a snare drum. Add some fancy dress costumes for an end of term performance—come as your favourite film character!

Extras

Cowboy song

A melody with simple ostinato parts which can be taught by ear or by rote.

Warm up 1: Teach everyone the two-bar ostinato (Part 2); violas, cellos, and double basses play in octaves, the violin part is slightly different. Play the two-bar phrase and have everyone echo what you play, repeating it a few times until it feels secure. If appropriate to your group teach the harmony parts in the same way.

Listen out: Make sure that the bow directions in the melody are observed and semibreves are held for their full length.

Performing: As the piano doubles the harmony parts and Part 2 any of these parts are optional, but make sure you cover the harmony and osinato backing somewhere. There are many ways to build up a performance. At its simplest, play the ostinato through twice as an introduction, then add the melody, then play out the ostinato with a fade ending. Alternatively, play the parts in all kinds of scorings and combinations to create something much bigger (and see Ideas for another suggestion).

Ideas: Try playing the melody in canon. Do this first at a gap of two bars and then try with a one-bar gap. With both options you can play with Part 2 (all instruments). Experiment with different dynamics. Try the ostinato pizzicato.

Backing track: This matches the performance track with the format: four-bar intro, melody once through, melody once through in canon (at two bars), outro. Effectively, the backing track thus allows for two statements of the melody, with or without canon at different gaps, plus an intro and outro.

Banuwa

An African round with a gentle syncopated rhythm. The repeated rhythmic pattern and its simple melodic structure built around an arpeggio make it a good piece to teach by ear or by rote. Once the melody is secure it will work well as a three-part round.

Warm up: Play the two bars of the ostinato phrase (Part 2) and have everyone echo back what you play. Teach the melody by ear two bars at a time in the same way.

Listen out: Be sure that there is enough bow for the tied quaver and minim at the end of each phrase. Make everyone listen to all the parts moving together when playing it as a round. Pointing out that the rhythm is the same will help make everyone aware and focus their listening.

Performing: The piano part is optional and provided simply in case a lead from the piano is required. With strings, play in unison first then split into parts for the round. The ostinato makes a good introduction. Encourage your players to suggest other ways of playing this piece. If space allows, processing from the back of a hall to the front can be an effective start to a concert. The cellos and double basses will have to stay seated!

Ideas: A simple rhythm on bongos or African drums would add some colour. When the melody is well known, try it by ear in another key; the melody works in G for all instruments using the same finger pattern (violins don't have a C string for the ostinato, but could finger the note an octave higher). Alternatively, try a different finger pattern, e.g. the key of C, starting with first finger on the D string.

Backing track: This matches the performance track with the format: four-bar intro, melody once through, melody twice through in three-part canon, four-bar outro. The backing track is 30 bars long.

Sea Suite

1. Shark attack!

The parts are notated with a 2 sharp key signature.

2

3

2. Barrier Reef

* Viola and cello part 2, bar 5 etc.: pizz. G D A open strings.

3. Cap'n Jack's Hornpipe

Jazz Suite

4 ○ 18

4. Simple syncopation

11

5. Feelin' blue

The parts are notated with a 2 sharp key signature.

String Time Joggers

14 pieces for flexible ensemble

piano accompaniment book

Kathy and David Blackwell

Contents

MUSIC DEPARTMENT

OXFORD
UNIVERSITY PRESS

Sea Suite

1. Shark attack!

The parts are notated with a 2 sharp key signature.

Printed in Great Britain

OXFORD UNIVERSITY PRESS, MUSIC DEPARTMENT, GREAT CLARENDON STREET, OXFORD OX2 6DP

2. Barrier Reef

* Viola and cello part 2, bar 5 etc.: pizz. G D A open strings.

3. Cap'n Jack's Hornpipe

9

Jazz Suite

4. Simple syncopation

5. Feelin' blue

The parts are notated with a 2 sharp key signature.

6. Broadway or bust

15

Jamaican Suite

7. Tinga Layo

West Indian Trad.

8. Jamaican lullaby

Jamaican Trad.

9. Kingston Calypso

20

Hollywood Suite

10. Spy movie 2

11. Sad movie

12. Action movie

Extras

(13 / O / 27) **13. Cowboy song**

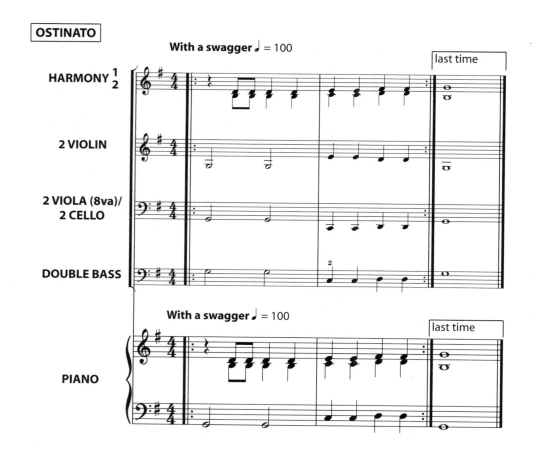

* The melody can be played in canon, the second part starting after one bar or after two bars.

14. Banuwa

MELODY

African Trad.

OSTINATO

PIANO PART

African Trad.

* The melody can be played as a three-part round, subsequent parts beginning at the asterisks.

6. Broadway or bust

Jamaican Suite

7. Tinga Layo

West Indian Trad.

20

8. Jamaican lullaby

Jamaican Trad.

9. Kingston Calypso

Hollywood Suite

10. Spy movie 2

28

11. Sad movie

12. Action movie

Extras

13. Cowboy song

MELODY

OSTINATO

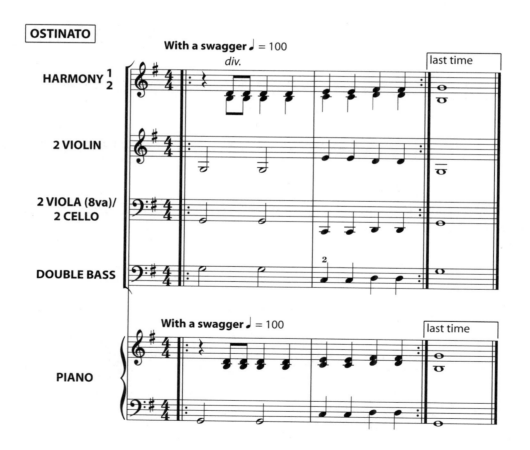

* The melody can be played in canon, the second part starting after one bar or after two bars.

14. Banuwa

MELODY

African Trad.

OSTINATO

PIANO PART

African Trad.

* The melody can be played as a three-part round, subsequent parts beginning at the asterisks.